Praise for
The Essential Coaching Leader

"Patty, your amazing interactions with these extraordinarily talented people was terrific—and so heartfelt to observe. [As we continue to partner together], our messaging and interactions are coming into focus and there are many topics to pursue. I'd do it again in a heartbeat."

—John Medina, Author of the *Brain Rules* Books

"The power of coaching can be a transformational and fundamental part of leadership. What I learned through Patty Burgin at SeattleCoach is that coaching allows the person you're working with to feel heard on a real and deep level and, through the power of questions, identify lightbulb moments that forward action in a profound way. I worked with Patty to bring coaching to a few select HR and Marketing leaders at Microsoft. These leaders then incorporated coaching into their day-to-day roles and made a significant impact on their teams and mentees. I loved hearing the positive feedback about their experience and I plan to continue the coaching philosophy and mindset at F5."

—Ana White, Executive Vice President and Chief Human Resources Officer, F5 Networks

"As a Leadership Coach, Patty is hands-down the most gifted person I have seen at facilitating meaningful conversations for groups. She holds people accountable to the impact they are having on others and helps them make movement as both individuals and teams. I couldn't write a strong enough recommendation for how much I admire Patty's skill and talent here."

—Astha Parmar, former Head of Global Talent at the Grameen Foundation and Founder and Principal at Inspri.co

"Helping others realize their dreams and potential is my purpose in my life. When I decided to add a coaching arm to my consulting business, there was only one choice of where to go: SeattleCoach. As part of Cohort #4, in 2008, I learned coaching skills that not only expanded my repertoire, but have since enabled my business to become one of the most rapidly growing consulting firms in the Pacific Northwest. Patty is a dream to learn from and I'm thrilled she is making her expertise available to everyone!"

—Amy Brown, Founder and President, SoDo Consulting

"Restless, ambitious, or poignant? If that sounds like you, read this book and share it with your team. These are Patty's hallmarks for people or teams ready to make a shift. Patty Burgin is hands down the best guide for integrating a coach-approach in organizational leadership. Her coach development process has been the most valuable leadership development I've done in 20 years as a non-profit and church executive. It makes a huge difference in our innovation, effectiveness, and hopefulness.

Those who think they've got this coach-thing mastered will learn fresh language and awareness. Those who wonder what in the world a coach-approach is will come to understand this dimension and when to engage it. If you just want to grow another step in your presence and effectiveness, soak in the attitude and hopefulness Patty shares."

—Corey C. Schlosser-Hall, Ph.D., ACC, Executive Director, Northwest Coast Presbytery

"I was exposed to the impact of Patty Burgin's coaching expertise when a direct report of mine took her course. I was amazed at the specific feedback her directs had on how she evolved her coaching leadership style as she took the class, and at how they began to develop and perform at an even higher level. This was a consistent message across her team. I was impressed. So when the next opportunity came up to take Patty's coaching course, I realized I had to make the time.

"Coaching is not what I was expecting. Patty taught me to 'coach the person, not the problem'. To me, coaching is about leadership. It is a different approach and skill set that can really empower the other person. The impact is longer lasting and the insights the person who is being coached has are reusable. As a coach, it is very rewarding to help others find their path in a way that is meaningful and personal to them. Patty provides tools and examples to which I continually refer as I become a better coach. In the middle of the program, my class cohort felt like we were not yet coaches. Patty disagreed. We were coaches now and we will continue to learn and progress to become even better coaches. I can't thank Patty enough for the tools, the experience, and the insights she shared. I, like my direct report, have become a better leader. And now, with all the leaders in our organization who have gone through the 'Coaching for Leaders' program, we are changing our organizational culture—helping others achieve more."

—Jennifer Marcou, General Manager,
Relationship Marketing, Microsoft

"Learning this content from Patty transformed my leadership. Not only did I become more skilled at helping people I lead to grow and develop, I also became more skilled as a parent and a facilitator of group learning. Turns out asking powerful questions that help others find their strength from within themselves is more engaging and effective than telling them what to do.

—Jane Gregg, Longtime Leader in High-Tech and Health Care

"After many years at Microsoft in people management, I have been inspired by a dramatic shift in our culture from a 'know-it-all' culture to a 'learn-it-all' culture. One of the key instruments of this cultural paradigm shift has been the art and capability of coaching. The journey for me in learning about the fundamentals, power, and inspiration of coaching began through the talented Patty Burgin and the training team at SeattleCoach. The experience has been both personal and professional as I have found coaching to be a calling that helps me to explore relationships in meaningful and impactful ways. Coaching rounds out a manager's capabilities beyond the typical practices of directing and mentoring employees. I see it playing a key role in building a team culture where employees feel like they can do their very best work. I am grateful to Patty and SeattleCoach for the investment they are making in developing our leadership capabilities."

—Steve Sirich, General Manager, Marketing, Microsoft

THE
ESSENTIAL
COACHING
LEADER

Also by Patricia Burgin

The Powerful Percent

The SeattleCoach PlayBook

The Coaching for Leaders PlayBook

THE
ESSENTIAL
COACHING
LEADER

The Brain-Friendly Practices for
State-of-the Art Leadership
in the 21st Century

PATRICIA BURGIN, M.A.
MASTER CERTIFIED COACH

PUBLISH
YOUR
PURPOSE
PRESS

For permission requests, write to the publisher, addressed "Attention: Permissions Coordinator," at the address below.
Publish Your Purpose Press
141 Weston Street, #155
Hartford, CT, 06141

The opinions expressed by the Author are not necessarily those held by Publish Your Purpose Press.

Ordering Information: Quantity sales and special discounts are available on quantity purchases by corporations, associations, and others. For details, contact the publisher at the address above.

Publish Your Purpose Press works with authors, and aspiring authors, who have a story to tell and a brand to build. Do you have a book idea you would like us to consider publishing? Please visit PublishYourPurposePress.com for more information.

Edited by: Karen Ang
Cover design by: Salman Sarwar
Typeset by: Medlar Publishing Solutions Pvt Ltd., India
Printed in the United States of America

ISBN: 978-1-946384-57-7 (print)
ISBN: 978-1-946384-58-4 (ebook)

Library of Congress Control Number: 2018966964
First edition, February 2019.

Dedication

*To Mom and Dad who showed me how to embark
on my charmed life.*

*To the Essential Coaching Leaders who have become a
part of SeattleCoach. You guys are showing the world the
brilliance of doing the craft and being the coach.*

*And to Dr. Kari who loves me and finds
so much fun along the way.*

Table of Contents

A Note from Patty

Since our first Coach Training and Development Cohort of aspiring professionals launched in May 2008, hundreds of seasoned leaders from scores of companies and five continents have joined the magic of SeattleCoach on Lake Union. We've trained and developed each one in small, face-to-face, interactive Cohorts, happily branding ourselves the "small craft brewery" of leadership coaching programs.

Some of our participants are entrepreneurs who are creating professional coaching practices. Many work in great companies as managers, leaders, directors, HR professionals, business partners—and now, as better bosses. Each one is becoming known as much for their personal ability and presence as a coaching leader as for the skills for which their companies originally hired them. They are transforming the cultures of their companies.

Sometimes there is an almost providential nature to history: Leaders appear, marked by the character and behavior required by their times—people without whom our story would be incomplete. Like the ancient Hebrew queen Esther who appeared just in time to become a hero to her people, I believe many of these coaching leaders may be appearing "for such a time as this."

From the Industrial Revolution and life before it to the pre-digital world of today's senior leaders to the current disruptive revolution in technology to our unfolding future with digital companions, human brains have remained relatively unchanged. We still have a preference for paying attention to one thing at a time and a responsiveness to personal connection, curiosity, and challenge. Everyone wants a boss who understands how to lead with those things in mind.

Life is big and life is short and it only moves in one direction. Each SeattleCoach has made me a better coach and a better person. And, along the way, we've built a shared vocabulary and mindset as coaches and coaching leaders.

Welcome to the story. Think of this little book as a brief introduction to a way of leading that is both ancient and new.

To the journey then,

Patty

Patricia Burgin, MA, MCC
Seattle, Washington

The SeattleCoach Definition of Coaching

A collaborative—even elegant—conversation, of any length, that fosters a growth mindset by inviting the full, dimensional intelligence and presence of the people involved. It is brain-friendly, highly customized, highly personalized, just-in-time adult learning.

Introduction

The Guy in the Window Seat

It was March 19, 2018, and I was flying to the West Coast from Washington, DC. The man seated between me and the window didn't take his eyes off the 35,000-foot view until somewhere over the Rockies. Then he turned and looked at me and said, "What a day, huh?"

I smiled back and nodded a little vaguely. Then after a moment I asked, "What do you do?"

He said uneasily, "I'm the CEO of a company that builds software for autonomous vehicles."

I nodded again, a little more knowingly this time. The night before, a woman in Arizona had been killed by an Uber car in self-driving mode. No one knew yet why it had happened.

Then the man asked, "What do you do?"

"I'm an executive coach," I said simply.

He rolled his eyes and said (rather loudly, I thought), "Coaches, coaches, coaches. Everyone's a coach!"

For a moment I thought about defending the honor and professionalism of coaches and coaching leaders everywhere. Then decided to instead just behave like a coach. "I know. There are more of us than there used to be. Are you headed home?"

Recovering from his little eruption, he nodded.

"What are you heading into?"

"My team is freaked out." He said quietly.

Maybe you identify with my part in this story. Maybe with the situation of the guy seated by the window. But, either way, if you see yourself in this story, here's what I know about you.

Like gifted leaders throughout history, I know that:

- *You love both support and challenge and that*
- *You are willing to experience discomfort in order to accomplish important things*
- *I know that you love it when you can connect and trust, and can be noble and grateful. Like other gifted leaders,*
- *You know that when we work—and even disagree— well with other people, it's satisfying and we learn better. I know that*
- *The demands on your time are not shrinking; people who respect and follow you want more—and more frequent—time with you. And I know that*
- *People-development maybe isn't what your organization hired you to do, but there it is. And, usually, HR thinks you're doing more of it than you really are. You want to get better at developing and retaining the talented people in your organization (without thinking you've got to be everyone's therapist).*

Why This Book. Why Now.

When someone like you starts to get interested in this "coaching thing" that has been getting so much attention in leadership circles, it's nice to have a solid introduction to the vocabulary and concepts of what it's all about. In the Pacific Northwest I do a lot of four-hour "Introduction to Coaching for Leaders" workshops. And they've caught on. Think of this book as a glimpse into the content of those workshops. (It's just less boisterous and experiential, with fewer demos. Sorry.)

Every time I teach a workshop for 40 to 50 leaders, a handful of them asks for more. And the options and opportunities I offer them are the same ones you'll find throughout this book.

So whether you just identified with me or with that good guy in the window seat, think of *The Essential Coaching Leader* as a brief introduction to some of the key whats and hows of coaching leadership. Or what I've come to think of as the world's oldest, newest, most brain-friendly way of leading.

Where We're Headed

If you're reading this, the world needs you to lead, and not just in your subject matter expertise. The coaches I've trained are engineers, lawyers, CEOs, surgeons, fitness experts, parents, pastors and faith leaders, entrepreneurs, consultants,

HR business partners, marketing experts, CPAs, recruiters, therapists, realtors, psychiatrists, teachers, business owners, and adventure tour leaders. And now they'll tell you they are also coaches and coaching leaders. And each one is finding an eager reception in a time when anxiety and loneliness are epidemic. Especially at work, where we all spend the majority of our waking hours.

What follows in five brief parts is what I've learned along the way about the best coaches and coaching leaders and how they find their magic in five Essentials: Their what, their where, their how, their big why, and, finally, their habit of staying curious about the question of what they could, should, might, or will do next.

Q_A *At the end of each "Essential" section of this book, I will offer an inquiry that I hope will help you to examine your own next step.*

Leadership Presence: The Coaching Leader's Approach and Why Brains Like It

"Vocation is the place where the work you most need to do connects with what the world most needs to have done."
—Frederick Buechner

"Lighthouses don't go running all over an island looking for boats to save; they just stand there shining."
—Anne Lamott

"Somebody has to be the grown-ups and now it's our turn."
—Dave Barry

Twenty years ago, after a decade of leadership with an international Christian nonprofit, I'd started a second act as a marriage and family therapist. And after a few thousand hours of listening to people, I began to notice that my favorite therapy clients were midcareer professionals who were say-ing things like, "I'm not anxious or depressed or addicted and my relationship is fine. I don't think I suffer more unfairness or injury in the world than anyone else, and when I fail, I have a good compass and I course correct."

And then, just when I thought they were ready to wrap up therapy, they would continue, "I know insurance won't pay for this, but I don't want to stop coming here."

The first few times this happened I'm sure I looked like a confused cocker spaniel. Squinting and tilting my head, I'd ask, "What would we talk about?"

Each one had this way of locking eyes with me and saying something like, "We would talk about my satisfaction and my contribution and where I'm headed in my life and work."

My favorite clients were restless, ambitious, and poignant. Some were in a personal wilderness. And I loved them. They taught me:

1. That midcareer is not a crisis. It's more predictable than that—almost like a second adolescence where you have a chance to wake up to more of your life, and
2. That the place where we spend the majority of our adult waking hours had better be marked by satisfaction and contribution. Or in the words of David Brooks, an Op-Ed columnist at the *New York Times*, "by two sets of virtues, the résumé virtues and the eulogy virtues."

My favorite clients had all worked hard at developing the skills and references on their résumés and for their LinkedIn profiles. And they were starting to think about their legacies—about their coming decades of work and about what would be said of them at their funerals. They taught me

3. That both lists of virtues matter to a life that is big and short and only moves in one direction. They were clear with me about their desire to consistently cultivate both lists.

My favorite clients didn't need a therapist. They needed a partner who would help them to explore what was possible and desirable, and then to shape a way forward into change or better performance—into their next chapter. They helped me understand the role of a professional coach.

Since, in my experience, good theology syncs with good psychology, I began to build a general "theology of coaching" based on the way Jesus interacted with people. I started coaching myself to:

- *Ask questions that were big enough to matter—and not just for gathering information—and then to wait for my questions land so that thoughtful people have time to reflect and choose rather than to answer automatically. I started coaching myself to*

- *Remember that the opposite of "lostness" and bad behavior is usually better connection. And to*
- *Be a continuous examiner of my own life and calling. What makes me a blessing? What makes me annoying? Where do I need to ask for help? And what belongs to only me to do? And I started coaching myself to*
- *Trust that grace is rarely intrusive and is usually disruptive.*

Like you, my points of view today come from each chapter of my life: as an organizational leader, as a systems therapist, and now as a coach. They also come from my lifelong attention to history and the resilience of societies that are guided by the most durably successful stories, virtues, creeds, and documents. Coaching is both ancient and brain-friendly and builds deeply on the possibilities that come with the cultivation of freedom, self-efficacy, predictable fairness, and the ability to find and integrate the points of view of good people.

And, by the way, there are a few things that coaching leadership is not:

- *An endlessly rosy belief in the radiant potential of human goodness. Nor is it*
- *A spiritual belief to "Let go and let God." It's not*
- *A mantra of exclusively happy thoughts and messages. Nor is it*

- *The elimination of any recognition of threat, challenge, weakness, or evil (cover ears, say la-la-la). And it is not*
- *Unexamined empathy that automatically supports and aligns with people who share your biases and is contemptuous of those who don't. Unexamined empathy usually fails to distinguish between offense and actual harm. Unexamined outrage is easy.*

The Coaching Custom

The story of Mentor comes from Homer's *Odyssey*. Odysseus, the king of Ithaca, is preparing to march off to fight in the Trojan War—and ultimately to a wandering, 10-year, well, odyssey. Before he leaves, he asks a wise older man to oversee his household and be a trusted advisor and protector to his young son, Telemachus. Odysseus commissioned the older man to, "Teach him everything you know." The wise man's name was Mentor.

In the roughly 3,000 years since the word *mentor* joined our common vocabulary, it has come to mean something like a trusted advisor, friend, teacher, and wise person who invests time, energy, and affection in the growth of another. And through the millennia, gurus, maestros, wizards, pastors, priests, guides, sages, counselors, philosophers, shepherds, wise advisors, heroes, reverend mothers, saints, exemplars, pilgrims, and Jedi Masters have joined and furthered the custom. Like any profession, there have been both geniuses and charlatans, but the best mentors have found ways to care, cure, support, and challenge. And through it all, the human appetite for secure engagement with the mentoring leaders whom we now call coaches has stayed the same.

Good jobs are not as standardized as they used to be. Training and development can't be standardized either. Organizational leaders who are succeeding in the 21st century know how to hone their curiosity, ask questions that are big enough to matter, and then listen responsively and behave resiliently—with their markets, their customers, their partners, and the talented people they hire.

Think of coaching as a way of partnering to create highly customized, collaborative, just-in-time adult leadership development. And here's the deal: That doesn't always have to be outsourced to external specialists like me. Leaders who have experienced coaching or who learn to coach begin to listen differently, to ask questions differently, and to keep a laser-focus on agreed-upon priorities, competencies, competitiveness, and performance. Their teams then join the learning. The results can be impressive and contagious, the return on investment (ROI) compelling.

Coaching leaders, even if they are not positional team leaders, help their teams to get better at both the whats and the hows of good work, including:

- *Their clarity about their shared mission*
- *Their understanding of the role of each team member's temperament, strengths, and growing edges*

- *Their ability to recruit, hire, on-board, and keep energetic talent*
- *Their ability to figure out the elements of structure and environment that will best support everyone*
- *Their steady focus on deliverables*
- *The continuous development of a growth mindset in both individuals and within the overall system*

The coach approach inspires people to bring their best in a way that telling, teaching, scolding, giving orders, prescribing, directing, rescuing, propping up, consulting, training, and nagging don't.

You probably wouldn't be surprised to know that top performance relies on compliance alone about 25 percent of the time.

A Brain-Friendly Intersection

My friend and occasional collaborator Dr. John Medina is a developmental molecular biologist at the University of Washington and author of the *Brain Rules* books. He studies things from the vantage point of genetics and molecules. I study things from the behavioral and the social. We're a good team, especially as we explore the following intersection.

Big, human brains have evolved to pay attention in a couple of big ways. Two parts are constantly jockeying over

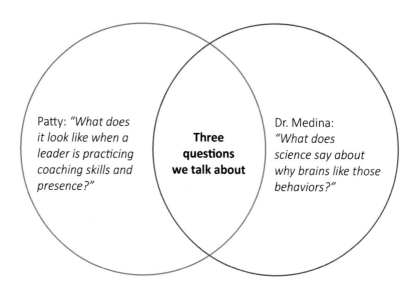

which part gets to run the show. One part is in charge of quickly assessing our environments, scanning for the unfamiliar and potentially dangerous. This part works automatically and serves the baseline goal of our survival. And since bad news is usually more sudden and dramatic than good news, you might say we're always looking for trouble.

Our brains have another way of paying attention. With the advantage of enough safety and predictability, the other part longs to solve problems, to create, to manage, to connect.

The cool thing about learning to coach is that you deepen your respect for and ability to work with both parts of human intelligence.

Until recently, the pace of change was slow and life was predictable. Threats may have been intense, but they were short-lived. Today, we wake up to an always-on world, marked by volatility, uncertainty, complexity, and ambiguity (a.k.a. **VUCA**: the trendy acronym coined by the Army War College in 1987).

A coaching leader helps people evaluate and prepare for change—to know when there really is a crisis or when it might be best to let things play out a little. She helps her coachees and colleagues to take an extra breath and to tolerate not knowing, to delay our reflexive and unexamined reactions—the ones that show up in the quality of our voices, in the depth of our breathing, and even in our expressions and postures.

Whether it's with an individual or a group or a team, a coaching leader helps people find the sweet spot between acceptable risk and challenge and the encouragement of acknowledgment and support. This dynamic is the place where people grow and flourish and become allies. This is usually done one decision at a time, one conversation at a time, one habit at a time.

Three Questions for Coaching Leaders

Psychologist Daniel Goleman, author of *Emotional Intelligence*, has an interesting critique of the popular "10,000-hour rule." He thinks it's "only half-true ... If you are a duffer at golf, say, and make the same mistakes every time you try a certain swing or putt, 10,000 hours of practicing that error will not improve your game. You'll still be a duffer, albeit an older one."

Drills and repetition might be part of arriving at leadership presence, or a coaching leader's approach, but moving toward mastery requires testing and learning and deliberate focus and course correction.

One of the great things for me about studying leadership presence and the coaching leader's approach with John Medina has been that he balances my incessant storytelling with an insistence on "the data." I challenge back with even more existential and compelling stories. He smiles and reminds me that his nickname is Dr. Grumpy and that a great anecdote supported by the data gets even more compelling.

Dr. Grumpy and I have identified three questions that live in the intersection of our harmonizing fields. Each one presents daily opportunities for coaching leaders. Each one appears daily in the minds of good leaders.

1. How can I precipitate more curiosity and compassion? Or is it empathy?

Whatever you call it, it's about perspective-taking and a willingness to be influenced. Sometimes it's about being a little bit less certain and a little more open to the experiences and convictions of other good people.

John summarizes some of his data on this question this way. At a high level, regardless of their temperament, effective leaders are able to do two things well: First, they make the trains run on time, and second, they are pastoral. That is, they are compassionate, moral, calm, and even inspiring. Would you be surprised to know that in John's research, people who work for leaders with just one (either one) of those attributes report about a 20 percent level of satisfaction? When the leader has both attributes, the level of satisfaction goes way up.

Here's how I interpret that data as a systems therapist and coach. There is a key concept from the family systems theory of human behavior that translates powerfully to organizational leadership. It is the core idea that the more a leader develops a clear sense of themselves, along with a healthy sense of their connection to others, the more calm, curious, and personally authoritative they become. They are more immune to passing criticism and emotionality and more positively and enduringly contagious. Even if they are not the positional leader, they may become the most influential leader on a team. This is at the core of how I see a coaching leader's presence.

Think of compassion as empathy plus a verb: the wisdom to do something useful. Compassion means you are simultaneously figuring out how to be separate and wise about your own life, while being connected to the lives of others. Compassion means you are interested in discovering what may need to happen next for the good of your team and its members. When compassion becomes a deepening habit, and a leader knows how to take an extra beat before responding, their behavior becomes more mindful and inclusive. Their personal course corrections become easier. And, by the way, no great leader is completely objective at all times. That's not even realistic. But the good ones are open to understanding their biases and patterns, and to learning from the people they lead.

If you're lucky, you've had a leader like that at some point in your life. Here's the second question that lives between John's brain-science world and my coaching-leadership world.

2. What ways of disagreeing solve problems and make things better?

According to John, it's not conflict that does the damage to relationships. It's the instability of unresolved conflict, where there is no psychological choice, little predictability, and no clear pathway back to civility and engagement. Not surprisingly, when parents fight in this way, their children (and of course their relationship) take the hit.

My corollary to John's research is that this remains true for us as adults in our lives at work.

Here's the other part of the data: The damage in disagreement also comes from verbal aggression and how it lands on us.

Whether it is snark or disdain or public shaming or yelling, or the worst show-stopper of all, contempt, there is a clear cost to individual and group or team functioning. When we're on the receiving end of verbal aggression, we involuntarily move into a state of wariness that takes time (John tells me that one study estimates two hours) to recover from. This is, of course, time stolen from productivity and learning and generative alliances (plus it affects fun and whether or not we look forward to going to work).

Here's what I know from thousands of hours with individuals, couples, groups, and teams:

We are never more unreasonable and unreachable than when we become afraid in a way we can't diminish.

- *We stop learning and experimenting.*
- *Kindness gets a little jammed up.*
- *We develop high blood pressure and need too much coffee to wake up and too much alcohol to relax.*
- *We can't stay asleep.*
- *We get frustrated that we can't create more order.*

I often ask members of teams what they learned growing up about how to engage in disagreement. I've started keeping a list of their answers. It seems like I hear as many stories about nervous silences, parental shushing, and angry standoffs as I do about wise parents who demonstrated how to take a deep breath and a step back and then to reengage with both clarity and curiosity.

13

"And now," I say to these good grown-ups (many of whom are now parents themselves), "Here you are on a team trying to figure things out." And then I point out that maybe God or the Universe has given them these people (I look around the room) as unique allies in a continuing effort to teach them how to have better disagreements. Sometimes they roll their eyes.

But it's true. A good coach or coaching leader can invite conversations that bring improvement, maybe even healing, to the automatic habits that most of us learned growing up.

And when brains find new ways to be calm and relaxed and engaged, they learn, connect, and perform better. They may even learn to disagree and to handle criticism better. And all of those hours we spend at work become more life-giving. Here's the third question that lives between John's expertise and my own.

3. What fosters learning and innovation? And how can other people help?

John and I were having lunch and talking about how it has become impossible in the past 100 years for any human brain to hold most of the knowledge that is known. I got curious. "John," I asked, "Do you think we'll ever have another Leonardo da Vinci?"

John thought for a minute and then said, "Have you ever thought about why humans are the most successful and dominant species? It's not because we have the longest teeth, the sharpest claws, or the thickest skin. Plus, we walk upright with all of our vital organs leading the way."

"We have big brains," I ventured.

John said, "We've thrived because we had the advantage of each other and we figured out how to work together to hold knowledge and information, to defend ourselves and reproduce, to solve problems, to respect boundaries, and, as societies, to create order, wealth, and beauty."

I don't know about more Leonardos, but the necessity of us working together in a world that is volatile, uncertain, complex, and ambiguous (VUCA) has become non-negotiable.

I came away from that lunch thinking about two things. First, we each carry around devices in our pockets that give us access to all of the knowledge in the world. More data and advice than Mr. da Vinci could have ever conceived of. This, of course, means that the price of advice is falling. And second, there will always be things that people who are restless and ambitious and poignant—people who see life as a stewardship—will do better than the machines. In a VUCA world that is easily manipulated and politicized, these are the people who will have the capacity for multi-directional curiosity and partiality.

What can a human-led company focused on long-run growth do better than a company led by algorithms? To be specific, what is it that only *you* can do? And how do we facilitate that? On a practical level, John's research gives us two simple data points about teams that learn and innovate well together:

- *There is conversational turn-taking. Teams actively agree on building the habit of balancing advocacy and inquiry. And the second data point?*
- *Women are part of the team.*

So, what fosters learning and innovation? And how can other people help? The coaching skill related to that question is the topic of Essential #3. But first, let's look at Essential #2 and at the world into which a great coaching leader steps into every day.

Sometimes I wonder what Odysseus recognized in the leadership presence of Mentor. My guess is that he saw the same foundation of character and cultivated wisdom that I find in many of my favorite collaborators and coaching leaders—men and women who are exploring the generative intersection between the coach approach and why the brains of the people they lead like it.

Q A *Think about your experience of being coached well in sports or in music or at work. In a word, what describes the person or partnership that comes to your mind?*

Essential #2

The Coaching Leader's Arena

"I focus leaders on themselves rather than on their followers, and on the nature of their presence rather than on their technique and 'know-how.'"
—Edwin Friedman

"I like to think that the C in CEO stands for culture. The CEO is the curator of an organization's culture…Anything is possible for a company when its culture is about listening, learning, and harnessing individual passions and talents to the company's mission. Creating that kind of culture is my chief job as CEO."
—Satya Nadella

"Management is about coping with complexity. Leadership is about coping with change."
—John Kotter

"You rarely have time for everything you want in this life, so you need to make choices. And hopefully your choices can come from a deep sense of who you are."
—Fred Rogers

Here's the dilemma for most new managers—and for some veteran managers as well.

Your company hires you for your subject matter expertise a.k.a. SME. And with the emphasis in the workforce on science, technology, engineering, and mathematics, a.k.a. STEM, your SME is likely to be knowledge-based and cognitive. Then, within a few years, you've become one of the best in town at applying your SME to products and services. So good, in fact, that your company wants to multiply your influence. So they give you a team of people. And you think, "I'm great at giving strategic and tactical direction. How hard can this be?"

And then you find out that your team members also look to you for noncognitive skills (e.g., listening, persisting, connecting, learning, and adapting). Your team also notices your character and resilience. They expect you to give direction, but they also expect you to mentor, inspire, teach, sponsor, and coach them as they grow in their own careers. And then you remind yourself that people join great companies and quit bad bosses. No pressure.

Noncognitive skills aren't soft, they are professional. And we are entering a time when the demand for them is expanding. David Deming, professor at the Harvard Kennedy School observes, "Work, broadly speaking, has shifted toward an emphasis on things we can't do with technology. There's no way to program a robot to figure out when a customer has had a bad day."

The Coaching Leader's Arena: Four Quadrants and Two Realities

You know how a great driver in a great car shifts smoothly through the gears, hitting the right one for the right conditions at the right moment? That's how I see the world into which coaching leaders step every day—a great coaching leader moves around what I call the Coaching Leader's Arena: in brief conversations; in meetings with individuals, groups, and teams; and in full coaching sessions that focus on the agenda or performance of their coachee or employee.

Based on my years of coaching and training smart people, here's how I've organized my thinking about the gears—the Coaching Leader's Arena, i.e., the world into which leaders step every day. Take a moment to let your mind wander around the quadrants below.

First, look at the north-south line. At the southern end is your SME—your expertise and experience. Maybe the stuff

*the **essential** coaching leader*

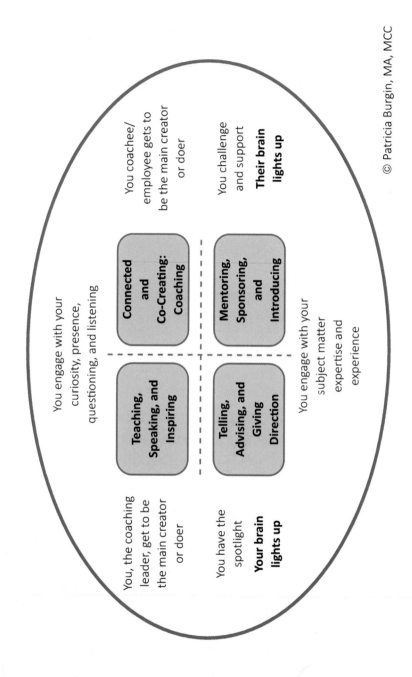

© Patricia Burgin, MA, MCC

20

for which you are professionally known. At the northern end is your ability to engage with curiosity, with good listening and great questions.

Next, look at that horizontal west-east line. At the west end, you get to be the main creator or doer. This is where you get to have good ideas and they get acknowledged! You love the west end because your brain lights up. But here's the deal: At the east end your coachee or employee gets the spotlight. They get to be the main creator or doer. You challenge and support, but they get the credit. You hear more "I-coulds" from them than they hear "you-coulds" from you.

Now focus on the labels of each quadrant. Each one is essential in the work of a thoughtful leader. From that southwest corner, leaders tell, advise, and give direction. From the northwest corner, they teach and inspire, from the southeast corner, they mentor and sponsor. And from the northeast corner, they coach.

Most managers and leaders have a quadrant that is their "default" gear—for many new managers, it's that southwest quadrant. And while they continue to grow in their expertise and experience, giving strategic and tactical direction and "coping with complexity," maybe they also learn to ask questions that are big enough to matter. And then they learn to listen for the meaning and possibility that come back to them from the members of their teams. They usually hear deepening levels of intelligence and possibility and enthusiasm. Maybe their impulse to micromanage diminishes. One coaching leader observed, "People seem more confident when I coach them than they do when I mentor them."

But coaching leaders also have to consider two realities that inform their progress as they work from the right quadrant for the right conditions at the right moment.

Reality #1 (The Surrounding Blue Circle): That's Your Personal Presence

As you decide which quadrant to lead from, it is your personal presence that will energize your decision.

The coaching leadership presence we talked about in Essential #1 (and will return to in Essential #5) is the foundational element to whatever gear you select. It includes your ability to be calm, confident, resilient, and authentic. It boosts your ability to move thoughtfully and fluently around the Arena as you do your job.

The more you become clear about what could be most useful in each moment for the individuals and teams you lead, the more you open the possibility of leading from the powerful gear of that northeast corner, which, as your team matures, may become a new home base.

No matter your starting point, it takes a personal pause button in order to be deliberate about when and how to move

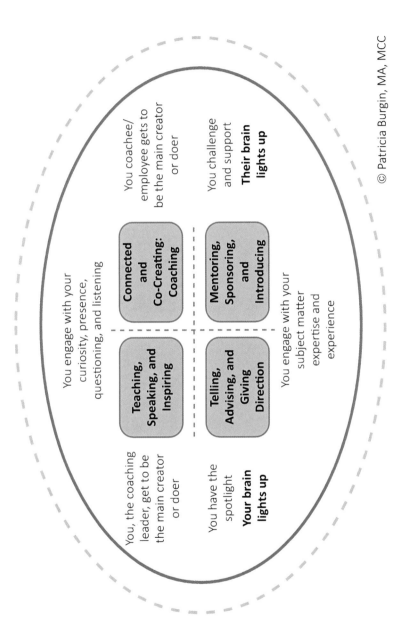

You coachee/employee gets to be the main creator or doer

You challenge and support
Their brain lights up

You engage with your curiosity, presence, questioning, and listening

| Connected and Co-Creating: Coaching | Mentoring, Sponsoring, and Introducing |
| Teaching, Speaking, and Inspiring | Telling, Advising, and Giving Direction |

You engage with your subject matter expertise and experience

You, the coaching leader, get to be the main creator or doer

You have the spotlight
Your brain lights up

© Patricia Burgin, MA, MCC

into each quadrant. Every leader I work with has their own defaults to recognize, to use, and to grow from. For example:

- *Do you have a bias for action?*
- *Is your bias for reflection and contemplation?*
- *Is your bias more for challenge or do you just love to support?*
- *What is important to you right now? (Performance? Business results? Employee development, satisfaction, and retention?)*
- *If you are deciding to learn more about the northeast quadrant, how will you experiment with and even talk to your team about your forays into the northeast quadrant leading as a coach?*

Here's what I've noticed about executives who get good at coaching: They learn to move around the quadrants as needed, without ever abandoning their coaching presence. And, over time, they have an impact on both the present realities and the potential of the organizational culture within which they work.

Reality #2 (The Surrounding Gold Circle): That's Your Organization's Culture

Organizations have their own defaults.

In the words of Satya Nadella, Microsoft's transformative CEO, there are "know-it-all cultures" and there are "learn-it-all cultures." And both bring a compelling context. I'm old enough that the companies I choose to work with foster both coaching presence and time to learn the skills required of leaders who invite conversations in the northeast quadrant—even brief ones.

A few years ago, I was contacted by a big company in Silicon Valley. They'd heard about the work I was doing in the Pacific Northwest. "We've got twelve young new executives whom we're investing heavily in," they explained. "Could you fly down and spend the day with them? Tell them a little about coaching?"

"Sure!" I enthused. "I'll need a big, open room with windows, an executive sponsor who can join us for the day—and I'll send down a few ideas for them to start thinking about. The sponsor is important—I'll be inviting a lot of interaction and your young leaders need to know what the bosses are thinking about coaching leadership."

Maybe I should have been nervous when, three weeks later, I hadn't heard anything further—except for an email confirming the time and place. Then, the day before our meeting, my executive sponsor emailed to say that another commitment had come up for her. "You know, Patty, we bring in a new expert for these guys every month and they are always eager to listen. I really can't be there, but my assistant will help you find the room."

Then I did get nervous. I flew down for the day and found my way from the San Jose airport to the right building and the assistant met me and led me to a small, low-ceilinged, oblong, windowless room that was oriented to a big screen at one end. It was dark.

"Hey," I said, "I'd asked for a room with more light and some open space!"

"Sorry," said the assistant. "This was all that was available." And then she left.

Luckily, I did have a few slides, so I set them up. And then in walked my audience of earnest young executives with their devices out, ready for some serious note-taking.

Over the next three hours I did my best to introduce and illustrate some key concepts, but nothing I did seemed to bring interaction, evaluation, challenge, or even much curiosity. Even though I'd asked them to put away their devices, they stayed intent on taking notes.

We wrapped up, everyone thanked me, and filed out. I called for my ride back to the airport. Then I sat on the curb in front of the building waiting and blaming myself. That insulting little heckler that lives in most of our heads got busy. I'd brought my calm authoritative presence and some good content. What had gone wrong?

In retrospect, I think I'd encountered a culture that was mostly operating, at least at that time, in the southwest quadrant. It was a "know-it-all" culture and was developing its emerging leaders accordingly. Maybe I'd influenced them a little, but the missing experience with an executive sponsor who had some fluency with the Coaching Leader's Arena likely influenced them a lot.

In the years since, when SeattleCoach builds a partnership with a company, it's not simply to do trainings. Rather, it's to come alongside visionary leaders who are building learn-it-all cultures. Leaders who understand the ROI of being able to move fluently around the Coaching Leader's Arena.

A Few Common Scenarios

Assuming you are calmly operating from your leadership presence, and that your organizational culture supports you, which part of the arena would you move toward in the following scenarios?

1. There's a deadline looming, and your most resource-ful team members ask for some clear direction from you. It's part of your job.

2. You've just promoted a talented young leader and part of her job will be to do more presenting and facilitating with customers. She worries, "I haven't done much of that. But I want to—I really want to get better."

3. A colleague asks, "Would you be available to come talk to my team about [your SME]?" You develop some

great content and build in time for your participants to interact over and to even evaluate what you present. They want to apply your wisdom.

4. Someone asks if you've ever navigated something like the tough thing they're facing and, though you don't talk about yourself much, you decide that it might be in their interest to share part of your own story with them.

5. Your employee asks for your advice but you have a hunch that he knows more than he thinks he does about what to do next.

6. Your colleague arrives from an emotionally intense day and can't remember what he wanted to talk about with you.

I've found that most leaders have a lot of familiarity with the northwest, southwest, and southeast quadrants. They call me when they want to build fluency with the key skills of the northeast quadrant. That's the focus of Essential #3.

Q A *Two questions for you as you consider the Coaching Leader's Arena: Which quadrant (or gear) is the "default" from which you've mostly operated? Which quadrant does your organization prefer you to use? If you made a 10 percent shift in the direction of the coaching leadership quadrant, what would your experiment be? And with whom?*

Essential #3

The Coaching Leader's Key Skills

"Coaching is the probiotic in the belly of the beast."
—Jennifer Winick

"Go into life and work thinking, 'Hit the ball to me!'"
—Bruce Larson, longtime Seattle minister and mensch

"We went to expose ourselves to fear and interrogate it."
—Elena Ferrante

"God became a human being and lived among us ...
He (approached life with both) grace and truth."
—The Apostle John

"The mind is not a vessel to be filled, but a fire to be kindled."
—Plutarch

"I'm always ready to learn, although I do not always like being
taught."
—Winston Churchill

My best teachers have always been my coachees. I've already told you about the men and women from long ago who explained that they "didn't want to stop coming here." It happened so often that I wondered if they were in cahoots. And then I started listening and learning and being influenced.

A few years later, another group of my favorite clients had a new request: "How do I learn to do what you do?" In retrospect, these were men and women who already understood the power of their leadership presence. And, at some level, they knew the limits of operating exclusively from the southwest quadrant.

Now they were ready to learn the core skills and competencies of professional coaching.

The first few times this happened, I said, "You could go to California. They train coaches in California. Or you could go online (where I'd done my coach training a zillion years ago)." But my best teachers kept asking me.

There is a much-quoted moment from Ernest Hemingway's *The Sun Also Rises* in which a character explains how he went bankrupt. "Two ways," he says. "Gradually and then suddenly." We've all experienced it. Physics calls it the *tipping point*. A Buddhist proverb says, "When the student is ready, the teacher will appear." Jesus talked about acquiring "eyes to see and ears to hear."

So, both gradually and then suddenly, I started teaching my favorite executives and their companies to coach. Essential #3 is my brief overview of the key concepts, competencies, and processes that are required of a leader who is learning to operate in the northeast quadrant.

It Starts with a Trusting Alliance

Coaching leaders attract people who want to grow and learn and get better—and to produce better business results. If you are learning the coaching leader's approach along with a little brain-friendly wisdom, and if you are figuring out the Coaching Leader's Arena, people want to work for you or with you. And, as you build trust, you earn the right to support with grace and to challenge with truth. This is where Dr. Grumpy would ask to see my research which, so far, is purely observational. So you'll have to take my word for it.

Here's What Happens Next

The first question any good coaching leader will ask you is some version of, "What are you ready to work on, leave behind, do more of, do less of, or get better at? What needs to happen next?" You may get responses from more than one area of your coachee's life, and their spouse or boss or team members probably all have their opinions. And if the person you're coaching works for you, you probably want to weigh in too on the outcomes and deliverables that matter to your own success.

Most people who are restless to grow and learn know they are on the threshold of change, that they are in the middle of it, or that they are settling into a new normal. Gradually then suddenly. *Suddenly* can be a quiet dawning or a jarring moment of truth. It can happen in your own awareness or, if you wait too long, it can slam into you from the outside. It can be an epiphany or a moment of dread or just a quiet conviction that something must change or grow or die. For example:

- *Gradually, I've taken on too much at work and all of a sudden, (a) I'm mad or (b) I'm exhausted or (c) they're not getting my best or (d) things are imploding*
- *Gradually, I've wanted to volunteer more and, out of the blue, this nonprofit comes looking for me*
- *Gradually, I've put on weight and all of a sudden, my chest hurts*
- *Gradually, what I really want to do more of/less of in my work has come into focus*

The playwright Lillian Hellman said, "Nothing, of course, begins at the time when you think it did." The beginning of change can be sudden, or it can take years. Sometimes when I ask, "What do you want to work on?" I hear a hunch, an idea just forming. Sometimes I hear a clearly defined commitment. An author I coach is beginning work on a new novel. She's researched 1840s Scotland, developed some fascinating characters, and written some vivid scenes. And she's told me that she's getting increasingly committed to the reality of this epic novel. In her words, "I'm not married to it yet, but I'm not seeing anyone else." She's steadily, creatively on the move.

Another client said recently, "Gradually, I've gotten restless in my work. I really like my employer and I don't want to leave. But I know I'm capable of far more contribution and satisfaction. I've thought about hiring you for a while and this is the right time."

In the four months that followed, this coachee and I met together 10 times. He took a hard look at a gradual and unsatisfying trend in his life and work and then he began to bend the trajectory of his life into a new direction. He found a new job at the same company—a far better fit. And, along the way, he clarified and learned to talk about *what* he wanted (more of, less of, same as) and *how* he wanted to begin showing up with colleagues, new bosses, new teams, and even with his family. One afternoon I listened to a sad update about his not being selected for an attractive project and (because we trusted each other), I pushed him a little, "It sounds like you might have to raise your game." Another time, I wondered aloud if he might need to go back and apologize to a colleague.

Then this note came from him: *I am super excited to move into this role—and I cannot thank you enough for everything that you did to help me get to this point. Without your coaching I feel I would have been spinning in circles trying to decide what I wanted to do, bringing more frustration to myself and my family.*

He's very gracious and I'll enjoy working with him any time he reappears with a new coachable issue. Throughout our months of work together, he was the expert on his own life. I was the expert at helping him to wake up to what he was starting to be ready for. I helped him to examine and test what could happen next: What to expect and pay attention to, how to hold steady in the process, how to think about obstacles (both the real ones and those little hecklers and resisters in his head), and how to talk about everything along the way—to colleagues and to his wife and family. Here are some other answers that have come in response to, "What do you want to work on?"

- *I want to be more inspiring and compassionate.*
- *I'm not sure. I'm in a bit of a wilderness.*
- *I need a new job—maybe find a better fit.*
- *I've got this new job and my deliverables inspire me—I want both them and my team to be world class.*
- *I've got this new team ...*
- *I want my team of veterans to work together better.*
- *It's time for me to write something.*
- *I have to give a keynote address to 1,000 people!*
- *We're having a baby.*
- *The last baby is leaving home.*
- *I need to make more money without losing my soul.*

I may hear about an emergency or a hunch or an upcoming challenge or a dream or a heartbreak or an idea that's just forming. As we explore and refine the agenda, the essential experiments begin to become clear.

And Then This Happens

As I get underway in a series of coaching conversations—even brief ones, I'm very aware of building on a three-part foundation: An alliance of trust (signal strength), clarity about the partnership's agreements, and a clear agenda. Without those things, you might be telling, teaching, scolding, giving orders, prescribing, consoling, directing, rescuing, propping up, consulting, training, and nagging. But you're not coaching.

A coaching agenda may include your coachee's or employee's focus, hope, destination, deliverable, outcome, or something they just want to get better at.

With a solid alliance, some generative exploration begins, and there is almost always a glance to what might or could or should happen next. New ways of seeing possibilities begin to emerge. What is the thing to reflect on or to experiment with? Or the calculated risk? The process isn't always very linear and includes everything from contemplation to planning to action. Sometimes you find out that what seems like a great idea is just not right for you. If it's not right, then why not? The answer might be where it gets brilliant. Something else— better, deeper, and unexpected—becomes clear. The process is about paying attention, exploring, testing, and learning in ways that are focused, clarifying, and well-paced.

Explore/Realize

You are actively engaged and curious.

Where do things stand now?
What does success look like?
What would the benefits be?
What would the evidence be?
For you?
For this organization?
What if you don't
make a change? Obstacles?
Strengths? Sponsorship?
Opportunities? Possibilities?

Awareness can be curative:
When you know, you can
do something.

Alliance

Agreements

Agenda

Find the Experiment/Next Step

**Your active presence
inspires initiative. Your coachee
begins to identify the next
possible and desirable
experiments and steps.**
What could you do?
What will you do?
Do you need a plan?
Who will know?
*What will happen between
now and the
next time we talk?*

Maybe the coachee figures
out what
they didn't know they knew.

Think of a coaching conversation, even if it's brief, as having not only a fulcrum of an alliance, an agreement, and an agenda, but an arc or a courageous rhythm between exploring and finding the next step.

Take a moment to reflect on the diagram on p.36. See if you can imagine a back-and-forth conversation—even a brief one–that could move between the questions under "Explore/ Realize" and those under "Find the Experiment/Next Step."

The Coaching Leader's Presence and the Core Four

Remember the blue circle around the Coaching Leader's Arena? It is the personal presence of the coaching leader that fuels the explore-experiment rhythm of a coaching conversation.

We all know people who grew up in tough circumstances. That was my father's childhood. For their own reasons in the midst of the Great Depression, neither of his parents were in his life much after the age of 10. But my dad had a compass that pointed him to a good grown-up who stepped in. The local pharmacist, John Leach, hired him to stock shelves, encouraged him to stay in school, and to learn photography. My father graduated, became a pharmacist's mate in the Navy, and during pharmacy school met my mother. They started a medical supply company and in their 68 years of marriage, they changed our family tree, along the way teaching their children and grandchildren about optimism and resilience. And about being good grown-ups ourselves in the lives of others. Thank you, Mr. Leach.

Beyond anything else, that's what a good coach needs to be (no matter how old the coachee): A person who, as a life practice, is the architect of his or her own character, resilience, and enduring happiness. A good grown-up.

The leaders who have regular ways of reflecting and examining and being deliberate with their own lives and relationships are the ones who can bring a reliable coaching presence to the people around them. Like a neighborhood pharmacist in 1930s Portland, Oregon, they are gently contagious.

Through my years of helping good grown-ups to become coaching leaders, I've learned to look for four elements that foster both exploration and experimentation and keep the dynamic in balance. I call these elements the **Core Four**.

First, I look for behavioral respect. This shows up in the co-created nature of a coaching conversation. The simple act of asking permission adds an extra beat to a conversation and injects more predictability and choice. I will frequently pause and look at the person I'm coaching and say, "I have a hunch about that. Do you want to hear it?" I can almost see blood pressure go down as, predictably, they smile back, take an extra breath, and grant permission. Or not. After all, this conversation is a partnership in which we are both great at something.

Second, I look for how a coaching leader pays attention to everyone's energy—including her own. You know when you're hosting a special meal, you set the table with some care, and then, as everyone gathers around it, you do something to mark the moment? Maybe you propose a toast. Or say grace. Or maybe you simply smile at each of the faces looking at you as you begin and thank them for being present. It only takes a moment, but it's long enough for human brains to reset and focus and to know they belong. Similarly, at the start of a coaching conversation, a good coach-host takes time to mark the moment. My calm, welcoming, (hopefully) unhurried energy makes me contagious in a way that fosters safety and belonging, which leads to learning. And that same energy helps me to stay more observant. What's going on when someone's energy drops? When someone leans forward to emphasize a point?

Third, I look for how a coaching leader acknowledges the admirable. Even children know the difference between general flattery and true **acknowledgment** of their character, effort, behavior, and self-efficacy. This never seems to change with age. Sometimes a coaching leader just has to say what she sees. After sitting in on a new manager's team meeting recently, I looked at him and said, "I know how hard you've been working, how focused you've been. And this morning I think I got to see it reflected in the enthusiasm of your team." All I had to do was to say what I saw and he beamed.

And the fourth behavior I look for is listening. When you think about it, we move through our days listening at three levels. Level I listening is for our own self-focused advantage and information. Level II listening rolls out for the transactional and for acquiring data. Level III is for listening beyond the words. What's the meaning? The possibility in what is being said. Level III takes extra focus and attention—and it informs the quality of the questions we ask.

The second question in the Bible was spoken by God to Adam who was avoiding the conversation, "Adam, where are you?" The question wasn't for God's data collection. It was for Adam's reflection. Not to overdo the comparison, but when a leader learns to listen and to ask questions at Level III, he invites a conversation that might increase engagement and understanding, support, and even challenge.

I loved it when one our SeattleCoaches, Kathryn Bergmann said, "I'm moving from thinking I have to have a list of life-changing questions to just listening for the right questions to ask."

Did you spot my Core Four acronym? **R.E.A.L.** Respect. Energy. Acknowledgment. Listening. They are the hallmarks of a coaching leader who finds his or her way into the magic of that northeast quadrant.

 Who are the people who already trust you to mentor, support, and challenge them? How did you earn their trust?

Essential #4

The Coaching Leader's Compass: How to Soul-Search and Self-Coach Over Time

"To journey without being changed is to be a nomad. To change without journeying is to be a chameleon. To journey and be transformed by the journey is to be a pilgrim."
—Mark Nepo

"I think midlife is when the universe gently places her hands upon your shoulders, pulls you close, and whispers in your ear: I'm not screwing around. It's time."
—Brené Brown

"The big break for me was deciding that this was my life."
—Jon Stewart

"I insist on a lot of time being spent, almost every day, to just sit and think."
—Warren Buffett

"I quite like that I don't think I've done 'good enough' yet."
—Sir Paul McCartney (at age 76)

My life has been marked by serial enthusiasms. And along the way, I've learned to be a coach.

As a fourth-generation child of the Pacific Northwest, by the time I came of age in the early 1970s, I had enthusiastically embraced the spectrum of possibilities before me. I was a half-hippie, half-sorority woman, environmental activist. I was also beginning a life-long fascination with the best stories and leaders of classically liberal Western civilization. I knew America wasn't perfect, but I loved that it was above all, a great idea and that it knew how to course-correct. For comic relief, I dated cowboys. At Oregon State University in 1970, one could happily be and do all of those things simultaneously.

Picking up on the practices I learned from my adventurous and entrepreneurial parents, I was already testing and learning, paying attention to what I might want to say "yes" to next, to what was possible and desirable, and to who I might want to be. And, as I've learned to see my life as a stewardship, these practices have only grown deeper. When I take time to reflect, to soul-search, and to coach myself, reviewing the components of this Fourth Essential helps me.

If you've gotten this far, you may be starting to think about what specifically you are ready to get better at as a coaching leader.

Here's who I keep running into. Whether it's at my office on Lake Union in Seattle, or on-site at some of the Seattle area's business rock stars of this new century, I find people who are the best in the world at what they do. Through decades of education, experience, grit, and always-on hard work, they are thought leaders and team leaders. They are paid well, often more than they ever dreamed they'd be.

And still, they are restless. And it's becoming clear to them—to all of us—that most of us are going to live longer. We're being given a lot more time than our ancestors could have dreamed of. How will that change the career trajectory that's been in place for a hundred years? And what will it take for that reality to settle in as good news?

How do you figure out what you were made to do at this point in your journey? And how do you attend to your journey so your gifts and values and legacy are maximized? The English word *vocation* has grown a little coolly practical, but through the centuries, the Latin verb that inspired it, *vocáre*, has carried the essential meaning of being called to a specific kind of work, to a craft, or maybe as an apprentice to a master. For some, a sense of calling is a spiritual aspiration. For others, it's about fit, and about listening to your life enough to find the work you really are most drawn to. Maybe it's about that paradox we've all experienced when we look up from a day of exceedingly hard work and think about how effortless and energizing it's all been.

Theories abound about how one succeeds at this treasure hunt: Is it a divine epiphany? Or following your bliss? My theory is that it's mostly taking time to soul-search and self-coach, and to get useful feedback from good people. And then continuing to make room for the stuff you want more of, while becoming clear about what you want less of. It's a lifelong iterative process if you're paying attention.

Most of the restless leaders I work with see their lives as a deep stewardship too. They are serious about examining their gifts and abilities and motivations—and this question of their calling. From thoughtful millennials to midcareer professionals to the wise elders who regularly protest to me that they're *"not done yet!"* the people I work with are engaged in finding and refining their path for the limited number of years they have left on the planet.

As I partner with them, it helps to think of three core incentives and of the places where they intersect. Each circle is crucial and interdependent but, by itself, not enough.

Proficiencies

What is the work that, up to this point in your career, you've gotten pretty good at? Maybe you love it, maybe you love parts of it. What is the craft, the SME for which you are already known, even as you begin to embrace or consider the idea of

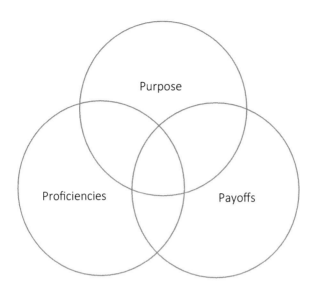

becoming a coaching leader? How does your SME inform your Level III questioning and listening? Could your SME help you introduce, explain, or illustrate ideas and then coach the people you most want to serve as they metabolize those ideas?

Purpose

When I was 12 years old, I noticed that Reverend Martin Luther King, Jr. did not say, "I have an idea." And I saw a person who, in the best possible way, was in love with his own life and with its God-given possibilities.

If the circle on the left is about your what, the circle at the top is about your future-focused and energizing why.

Maybe you notice it at the end of a very satisfying day in which you know you have contributed, served, and lived out your big values. You lost track of time a little. Maybe you lead an organization that employs hundreds of people who love what they do and act like its owners. Maybe you know you have developed or championed greater efficiency or order or delight, or created a team that just works well and happily together. Maybe your customers trust you, your focus, and your track record. You know that your example matters to all of them. You do the work well and you don't cheat. If you have a spiritual tradition or practice, your sense of purpose will feel aligned with it. There is almost always a connection between prosperity and having a clear sense of purpose or even a calling. Maybe you aren't one to follow your bliss, but you do keep it in sight.

Payoffs

The circle on the right speaks to what spells freedom to you. What does great compensation look like for you? A number probably comes to mind. Write it down. But also ask yourself, "Once the money is OK, how else do I like to be compensated?" Your answer is probably about being able to have choices and autonomy and the ability to explore and create and produce. Maybe you like a strong team with an affirming leader or being the boss or traveling a lot—or not, or being acknowledged publicly for your craftsmanship or making innovation practical or being trusted with a flexible work schedule. Maybe you're the one people come to with their hunches and hurts and with their own restlessness to get better at something.

Finding Your Experiment

As you become more acquainted with your True North—that's the evolving intersection—you begin to notice opportunities that appear. What do you think people would gladly pay you—or thank you—to do more of? What could you be one of the best in the world at?

Maybe you are paid well to do something that you're not getting better at or enjoying very much. Maybe you're eager to learn something new. Maybe you are ready to cultivate an area of potential mastery with which you've only experimented (but for which you've often been thanked).

If you like the work so much that in addition to the hours, you add focus, tolerance for failure, course corrections, and the risk required to increase your limits, your True North begins to emerge.

As we explore and attend to each one of the moves we make, the compass works, and our evolving sense of fit begins to resonate with satisfaction, contribution, service, and prosperity. As with any compass heading, where you start is not where you'll land, and course corrections are continuous.

Your intuition gets restless; you stop and check, and maybe backtrack or sprint. Or you stop to savor a spectacular vista.

To check your heading (or, if you prefer, your signal strength), start with your most personally compelling circle (purpose? proficiencies? payoffs?). The question you examine in your own life will help you identify what, at this moment in your life, you're ready to get better at. It will also build your ability to listen well to others and to ask them questions that are big enough to matter.

Q A *Two questions about your **Proficiencies**: What are the stories you love to tell about how you've gotten good at what you do? What still delights you about that area of mastery?*

*Two questions about your **Purpose**: What are the compliments that mean the most to you? Who do they come from?*

*Two questions about your **Payoffs**: Once the money is OK, how else do you like to be compensated?*

And what do you think the world would gladly pay you—or thank you—to do more of?

Essential #5

So What? Now What?

"The next best thing to being wise oneself is to live
in a circle of those who are."
—C.S. Lewis

What I know as a professional coach is that an interesting conversation becomes a real coaching experience when I start to hear about what your next possible and desirable step will be. Maybe you tell me you'll start to contemplate a new idea. Maybe you're building in time to start talking about your maturing vision. Or maybe you look at me and smile and say, "OK. It's time to make my move."

Think of the questions, "So what? Now what?" as Essential #5.

The people I coach figure this out. And, as my partnerships with them grow, they start beating me to it. I hear more "here's-what-I-could-do's" from them than they hear "here's-what-you-should-do's" from me.

So what about you? What do you want to get better at?

Here's what I love about people who are interested in growing as coaching leaders.

1. You're already great at something else: You've spent years learning your SME. As I mentioned in the introduction to this book, the coaches I've trained are executives, lawyers, engineers, CEOs, surgeons, fitness experts, parents, pastors and faith leaders, entrepreneurs, consultants, HR business partners, marketing experts, CPAs, recruiters, therapists, realtors, psychiatrists, teachers, business owners, and adventure tour leaders. And now they'll tell you they are also coaches and coaching leaders.

2. The second thing I love about people like you is, that though you may already see yourself as a mentor and servant-leader interested in the development of others, your interest in coaching implies that you're willing to be a learner again.

As I wrapped up one of my more in-depth SeattleCoach Cohorts at a transformative global company headquartered in the Pacific Northwest, I asked a bunch of executives-turned-coaching-leaders a question:

"Do you think this company of yours will make more money, have more fun, and do more good because you guys

have invested this time in becoming coaching leaders?"
(They all spoke at once)

- *"We'll listen better and take better risks."*
- *"We'll ask better questions and be more innovative."*
- *"We'll take criticism better."*
- *"We'll course correct faster."*
- *"We'll argue about the right things, but more kindly."*
- *"We'll probably stay around longer."*

(Then someone dropped a mic.)

Conclusion

Remember back at the beginning when I talked about my "Introduction to Coaching for Leaders" workshops? And how this book reflects much of that content? Below are the next-step options we suggest both at our workshops and now here, for you.

I bet one or more will sync with your own so-what-now-what. The QR code below will take you to the "Contact Us" page on the SeattleCoach website. From there, you can click a box or two and we'll get right back to you about any of the following options:

- *Personal executive coaching with me or a member of my team*
- *Bringing the SeattleCoach half-day workshop **"Introduction to Coaching for Leaders"** to your company*
- *Customizing a longer-form "Coaching for Leaders" program for leaders in your company.*
- *Professional coach training and development in the Seattle area. We offer the full International Coach Federation (ICF) credentialing track.*

- *Bringing complimentary organizational "lunch-and-learns" to Seattle-area companies. You bring lunch. We bring a generative and customized conversation about coaching leadership.*

As I like to say, SeattleCoach has become known as the small craft brewery of coach training and development programs in the Pacific Northwest. Everything we teach has been reviewed and accredited by the industry standard set by the ICF. And everything has also been approved by hundreds of SeattleCoaches who are having an impact on the West Coast and beyond as external coaches and as better leaders on the inside of great companies and organizations. Scores of them have been awarded international certification by the ICF.

If, as you've read *The Essential Coaching Leader*, something resonates, get in touch with us. You will be joining a big and important very cool conversation.

I'll say here what we say at the close of every SeattleCoach gathering. We stand in a circle, raise a pretend beverage, smile at each other and toast each other. With our very best Scottish accents, we proclaim, To the Journey Then!

The Last Word

From SeattleCoaches and Their Coachees

"The members of our company who have completed the program are showing up differently with their teams. They are both 'coaching leaders' and 'coaching team players.'"

"I feel like I have ramped much faster as a new manager than I would have had without it. In fact, I would say that I have learned in 4 months what would have taken me a year to learn."

"What continues to present itself is the wisdom of how you've designed this coursework. More than the rules and ways of coaching, it is heart and soul + science and framework. I love this mix."

"Thank you for helping me push myself down the road I always wanted to be on."

"The coaching mindset is an amazing skill when I'm coaching others and even just in my daily interactions, both professional and personal."

"Slowing down and asking questions rather than jumping in with your immediate thought is a good skill to have."

"I have gotten so much more from this experience than I anticipated. Not only do I think it will make me better at coaching, but I have been pleasantly surprised at how I am rethinking my leadership philosophy and approach because of this coaching training."

"The experience, the learning, the discussions with others in the class are so nicely aligned to what we want to see in the new version of Microsoft. In so many ways, this is aligned to the culture we want to create. I am honored to get this opportunity and wish others benefit from this experience and learning as well."

"This is the most consistently useful personal development activity I've undertaken at Microsoft."

"The sessions have helped me figure out how to move through work at a challenging time in my career and to make solid changes which are already having a positive impact on my work relationships, quality of output and career growth."

"From the first day I came here, I have had a sense of this being about my future, of both recognizing and creating what's out there for me."

"I think what I love the most about working with Patty is how she shined a light on my skills and accomplishments and allowed me to see them. Really see them."

"There are horse whisperers and there are dog whisperers. Patty is the people whisperer."

"Patty may not be a parent, but she's a 'mom' like Oprah is a 'mom.' She is a compassionate bad-ass."

"This has been way more than 'coach training.' My soul feels bigger."

"Patty is one of the best. High integrity, compassion, spirituality, smarts, and a keen sense of humor makes her the best coach trainer I've ever had the honor to meet."

"Thank you for answering your calling—and for helping us answer ours."

"You turn people into coaches! How do you do that?!"

"As I finish, I think I'm a better coach. I know I'm a better person."

"This is so much more than training. I've learned from listening to everyone else in my Cohort how to listen to myself better. It's a juicy growth opportunity."

"I love what I do in a way I never imagined was possible."

"There are juicy bits to your much-layered instruction that usually dawn on me as I drive home. There's science behind why this works. You don't regale us with some of the whys and wherefores, but are willing to go down the road when asked. Subtle genius ... Coaching training with you makes me a better person."

"My coaching comes into play daily, as I recognize how I can have better presence, ask better questions, and help to make the world a better place."

"The entire program has been a gift and I will be forever grateful for our thoughtful and quietly transformative sessions. You have dug deep to create something that the world so desperately needs and found ways to empower and encourage more and more of it. And now I'm part of it!"

"Here's what turns me on: People of compassion acting with courage, connected with their life calling (purpose). One person or team living this way can cascade into their families, friends, colleagues, congregations, neighbors, and fellow citizens."

"I see opportunities for the application of my new skills every day."

"I feel like I've learned to golf from Arnold Palmer."

"You can take this stuff and make it your profession. You can also make it your way of living. Date night is better. Parenting is better."

"Thank you, Patty, for following your vocation. You've opened a world of opportunity for other people to find their path. You have created magic."

SeattleCoach Best Reads

Alan Alda. *If I Understood You, Would I Have This Look on My Face?: My Adventures in the Art and Science of Relating and Communicating*

Kate Braestrup. *Here If You Need Me: A True Story*

Arthur Brooks. *Love Your Enemies: How Decent People Can Save America from the Culture of Contempt*

David Brooks. *The Road to Character*

Bill Burnett and Dave Evans. *Designing Your Life*

Dolly Chugh. *The Person You Mean to Be: How Good People Fight Bias*

Amy Cuddy. *Presence: Bringing Your Boldest Self to Your Biggest Challenges*

Ivan Doig. *Dancing at the Rascal Fair*

Carol Dweck. *Mindset: The New Psychology of Success*

Niall Ferguson. *Civilization: The West and the Rest*

Elena Ferrante. *My Brilliant Friend*

Barbara Fredrickson. *Positivity: Top-Notch Research Reveals the 3-to-1 Ratio That Will Change Your Life*

Edwin Friedman. *A Failure of Nerve: Leadership in the Age of the Quick Fix*

Daniel Goleman. *Emotional Intelligence*

Lynda Gratton and Andrew Scott. *The 100-Year Life: Living and Working in an Age of Longevity*

Herminia Ibarra. *Working Identity: Unconventional Strategies for Reinventing Your Career*

Johann Hari. *Lost Connections: Uncovering the Real Causes of Depression and the Unexpected Solutions*

Robert Kegan. *Immunity to Change: How to Overcome It and Unlock the Potential in Yourself and Your Organization*

Patrick Lencioni. *The Advantage: Why Organizational Health Trumps Everything Else in Business*

C.S. Lewis. *Mere Christianity*

John Medina. *Brain Rules*

Satya Nadella. *Hit Refresh: The Quest to Rediscover Microsoft's Soul and Imagine a Better Future for Everyone*

Peggy Noonan. *The Time of Our Lives*

A. Rafaeli, et al. "When Customers Exhibit Verbal Aggression, Employees Pay Cognitive Costs." (*Journal of Applied Psychology*)

Matt Ridley. *The Rational Optimist: How Prosperity Evolves*

Matt Ridley. *The Evolution of Everything: How New Ideas Emerge*

Marilynne Robinson. *Gilead*

Simon Sinek. *Leaders Eat Last: Why Some Teams Pull Together and Others Don't*

About the Author

As a leader, facilitator, speaker, author, and coach of leaders, Patricia ("Patty") Burgin has advised and mentored thousands of individuals and teams toward better performance, communication, and meaning.

Following stints in the international leadership of a Christian nonprofit, as a conference speaker, as a tour leader in the former Soviet Union, and as a licensed marriage and family therapist, Patty founded SeattleCoach® in 2003 and began to coach and facilitate exclusively in 2005. In 2008, she launched the SeattleCoach Professional Training and Development Program, which is credentialed by the industry-standard International Coach Federation (ICF).

Whether it's a class or a keynote, Patty values insight creation as the crucial component of content delivery. "I love it when my brain lights up," she says. "And it's even better when everyone else's brains light up." She works with an approach that is warm, practical, innovative, direct, playful, and generous.

She holds two masters degrees, one in Theology and a second in Applied Behavioral Science, and has joined the top 4 percent of credentialed coaches worldwide to have been awarded the title of Master Certified Coach by the ICF.

A native of the Pacific Northwest, Patty loves just about everything about it: the water, the coast, the mountains, the great IPAs, and *"not having to squint as much as Californians do."* During her freshman year at Oregon State University she was named "Smart Ass of the Year" by members of her sorority. She lives near the Seattle Zoo with her partner, Dr. Kari, a veterinarian, and with a revolving assortment of creatures.

With Patty's background as a competitive rower, and as past president of Interlochen Rowing Club in Seattle, she sometimes takes executive teams out on the water with her.

When a team sits together in a racing shell (60′ × 18″), the experience quickly produces soggy metaphors and boatloads of team learning.

Her faith still informs her life and work, helping her to explore how human brains and relationships flourish, how we make sense of the tough stuff, and how we live out those big what's-it-all-about questions that we share through the arcs of our lives. She thinks excellent coaching is like grace: rarely intrusive, usually disruptive, more nuanced than announced, and just as much about *how* as *what*.

Made in the USA
Monee, IL
03 November 2019

16242280R10055